1 2 3 4 5 6

Colorful Word Search

Search for the colors below!
Look up or down; left or right!

```
B A U K L A V E N D E R E
B R O W N V S T I L N E G
S G F E T I H W A K A D I
Z R B U B A D S A C U X E
Y E L L O W V B M A W R B
O E D B R A A T E L O I V
G N A T A Q U A A B U R N
I O W D N E P E K R D W Q
D C A A G D E S N
N S R P E A C H I
I V W E L P R U P
```

PINK
PURPLE
BLUE
GREEN
YELLOW
ORANGE
RED
VIOLET

AQUA
BLACK
WHITE
PEACH
LAVENDER
BROWN
INDIGO
BEIGE

5

Dreamland Dot-to-Dot!

Connect the dots to discover what's floating on a cloud!
Then color in your dreamland discovery.

Spot the Differences!

There are ten differences between these two ice cream cones. Can you spot them?

Missing Half!

This delicious ice cream sundae is about to melt!
Complete this illustration and then color in your delicious treat.

Word Scramble!

These animal names have become scrambled!
Help sort out the mix-up in the spaces below.

H L S T O

_ _ _ _ _

P A E L N T E H

_ _ _ _ _ _ _ _

M A L A L

_ _ _ _ _

R F G O

_ _ _ _

L N A M G I F O

_ _ _ _ _ _ _ _

R U T E T L

_ _ _ _ _ _

Color the Garden!

Finish drawing the flowers, and then color them in to create a beautiful flower garden.

Color the Unicorn!

A-maze-ing!

Help this unicorn find her way to
the magical rainbow!

START

END

12

Color by Number

Color this beautiful palace scene
by using the color key below!

Spot the Differences!

There are eight differences between the two uni-kitty gardens. Can you spot them?

Finish the Patterns!
These images form a pattern.
Can you complete the sequences?

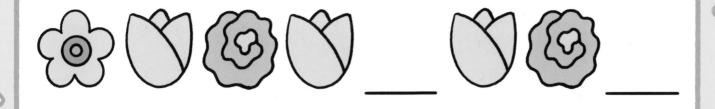

15

Sudoku

How quickly can you complete the grid? The same picture cannot appear twice in any row or column.

Color by Number

Color this underwater scene by using the color key below!

| 1 | 2 | 3 | 4 | 5 | 6 | 7 |

Learn to Draw Unicorns!

Follow the steps in red to draw
a unicorn head with flowers.

1.

To begin: Lightly draw these basic shapes. You'll erase them later on.

2.

Then: Follow each new step in red to draw this unicorn.

3.

4.

5.

6.

7.

8.

19

Find a Match!

Two of these cupcakes are exactly alike. Can you find them?

Animal Friends Word Search

Search for the animal names below!
Look up or down; left or right!

```
A Y L F R E T T U B
F L A M I N G O E U
O I F B J O W L Y N
U P C L A H W R A N
C A E A C Z D F A Y
A R H N T U R T L E
T S T N A H P E L E
F R O G V D L G A K
H W L C A M G O M W
X A S T N E L E A L
```

FLAMINGO   TURTLE   ELEPHANT
BUTTERFLY   NARWHAL   FROG
CAT   LLAMA   SLOTH
BUNNY   OWL

Underwater Crossword Puzzle

Use the numbered images to complete this crossword puzzle.

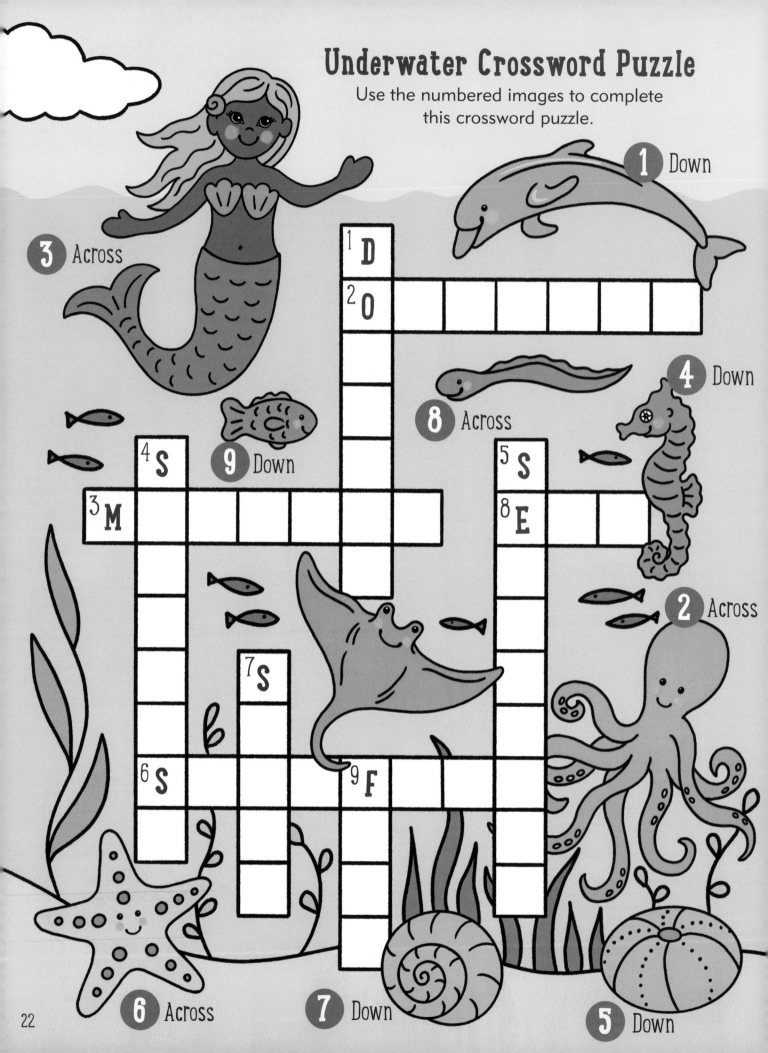

1 Down

3 Across

4 Down

8 Across

9 Down

2 Across

6 Across

7 Down

5 Down

1 **D**
2 **O**

4 **S**
3 **M**

5 **S**
8 **E**

7 **S**

6 **S**
9 **F**

Silly Strings

Follow the strings to connect each
flower to a bug!

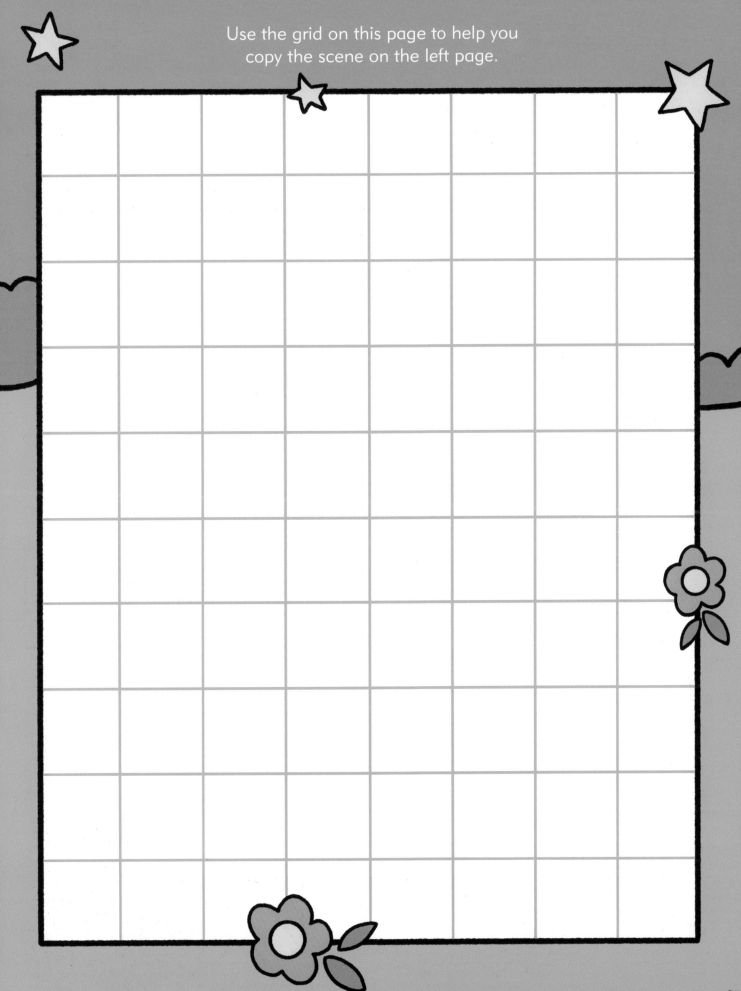

Use the grid on this page to help you
copy the scene on the left page.

25

A-maze-ing!

Help this unicorn find her way to
the treasure chest at the
bottom of the sea!

26

Color the
Outer Space
Scene

Royal Dot-to-Dot!

Connect the dots to discover what is beneath the rainbow! Then color in your discovery.

Finish the Portraits!

Finish drawing the unicorn portraits, color
them in, and name your new friends!

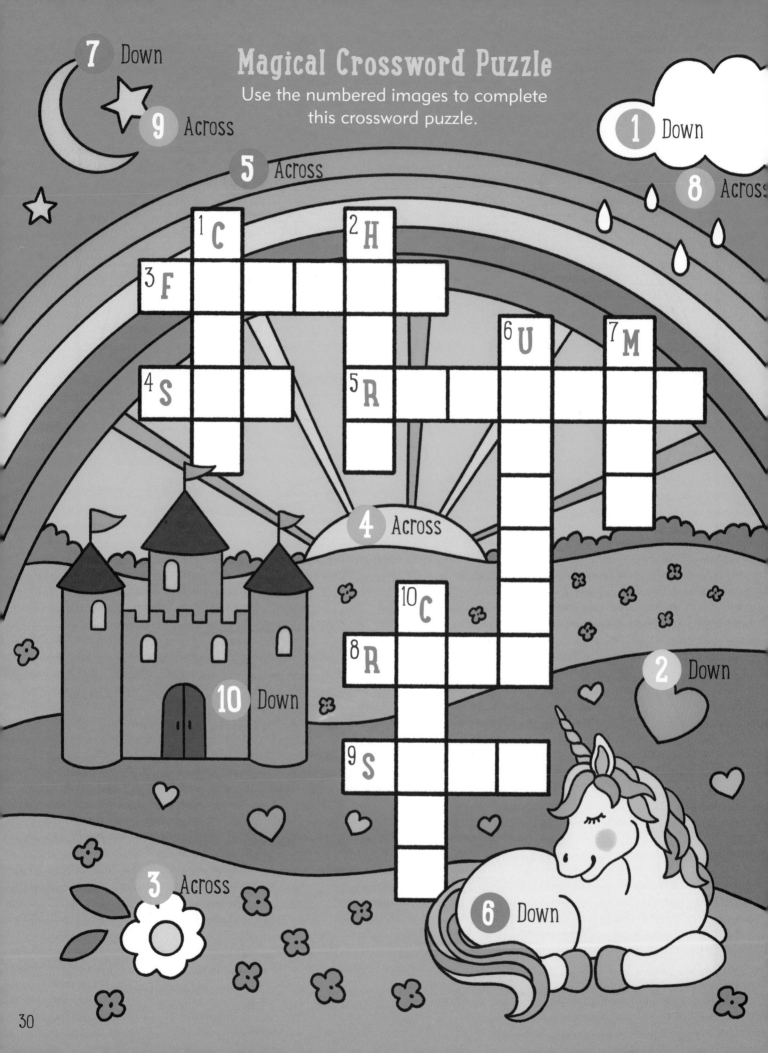

Magical Crossword Puzzle
Use the numbered images to complete this crossword puzzle.

7 Down
9 Across
5 Across
1 Down
8 Across

1 C
2 H
3 F
4 S
5 R
6 U
7 M
4 Across
10 C
8 R
2 Down
10 Down
9 S
3 Across
6 Down

30

Word Scramble!

The letters on these labels have become scrambled!
Help sort out the mix-up in the spaces below.

K A C P U C E

_ _ _ _ _ _ _

W A R B O I N

_ _ _ _ _ _ _

E C T L A S

_ _ _ _ _ _

E R T H A

_ _ _ _ _

R T S A

_ _ _ _

I M D M A E R

_ _ _ _ _ _ _

R F O L E W

_ _ _ _ _ _

Silly Strings

Follow the strings to connect each
unicorn to a cupcake!

Color by Number

Color this unicorn by using the color key below!

| 1 | 2 | 3 | 4 | 5 | 6 | 7 |

33

Spot the Differences!

There are eight differences between these two pictures. Can you spot them?

Complete the Drawing!

Finish the drawing and color it in!

What Do Unicorns Eat?

Find the words for these breakfast treats in the jumble of letters below!
Look up or down; left or right!

GRAPES

DONUTS

GRASS

PANCAKES

FLOWERS

BANANAS

```
B A F E R W U R S A
F O S A N A N A B S
O I E S E P A R G E
S P L R O D E P R I
E A P A C Z D F A R
I A P N C F A Y S R
K P A N C A K E S E
O D O N U T S N N B
O W A S R E W O L F
C E R E A L L H A L
```

BERRIES

CEREAL   COOKIES   HONEY   APPLES

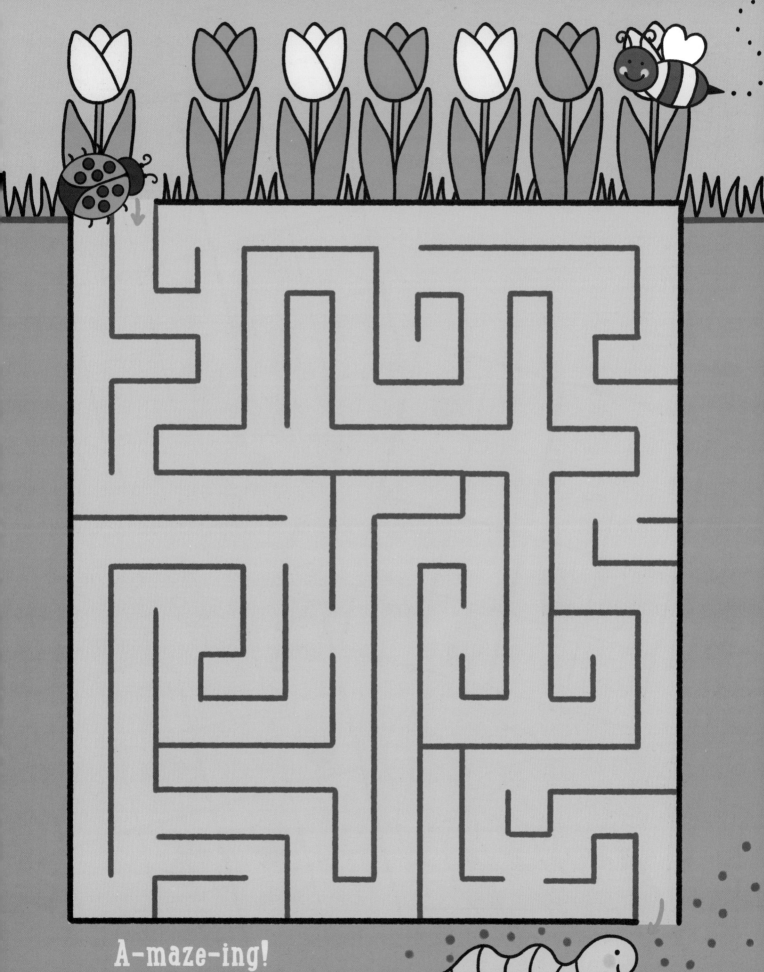

A-maze-ing!

Help this ladybug find her way to her friend the worm!

Sudoku

How quickly can you complete the grid? The same picture cannot appear twice in any row or column.

Find the Unicorns' Names

To figure out each name, find the letter that corresponds to each number/letter clue.

	1	2	3	4	5	6
A	T	A	X	Y	B	C
B	L	Z	W	C	R	E
C	R	F	O	L	D	M
D	H	Q	R	I	N	G
E	S	M	T	P	V	E
F	J	R	Y	L	N	K

C2	B5	D4	E1	F6	A4

B2	D4	E1	C6	A5	F3

	1	2	3	4	5	6
A	Q	R	D	U	I	O
B	V	O	N	A	H	P
C	G	W	B	T	N	V
D	F	J	S	L	D	E
E	I	C	Z	X	K	M
F	M	R	A	Y	N	L

Decorate the Cupcakes

Finish the drawing and color it in!

A-maze-ing!

Help this unicorn make her way
through the castle to find her friend!

Turn These Animals into Unicorns

Just add a horn!

Learn to Draw Mermaids!

Follow the steps in red to draw a pretty mermaid.

1.

To begin: Lightly draw these basic shapes. You'll erase them later on.

2.

Then: Follow each new step in red to draw this mermaid.

3.

4.

5.

6.

7.

8.

Spot the Differences!

There are ten differences between these two unicorn gardens.

Can you spot them? Then color the pictures.

Missing Half!

Complete this illustration and then add color.

Color by Number

Complete this unicorn scene by using
the key below to color her in!

1 2 3 4 5 6 7

49

Tasty Crossword Puzzle

Use the numbered images to complete
this crossword puzzle.

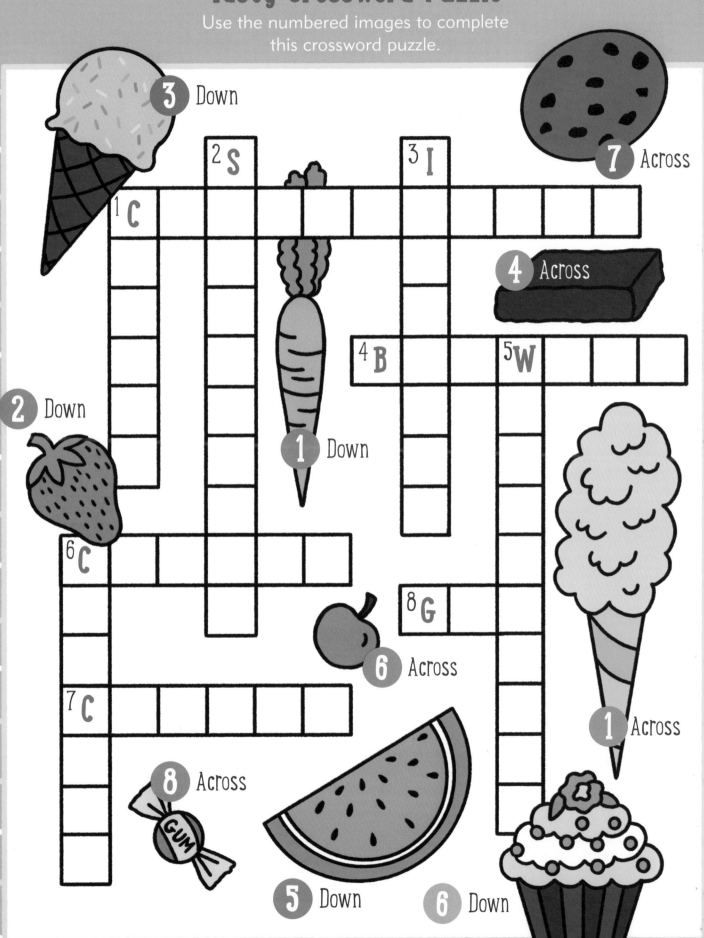

Learn to Draw a Castle!

Follow the steps in red to draw a castle.

1.

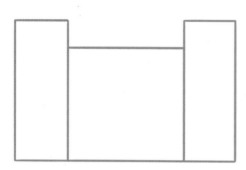

To begin: Draw these basic shapes.

2.

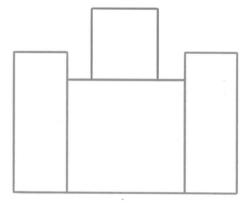

Then: Follow each new step in red to draw this castle.

3.

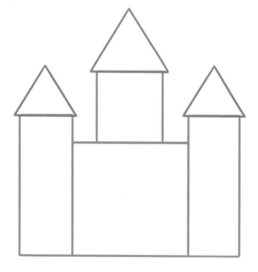

4.

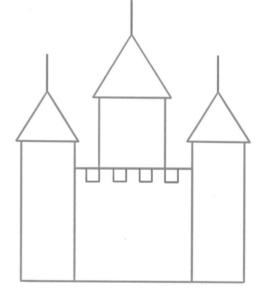

5.

6.

Fantasy Word Search

Find the words in the jumble of letters below!
Look up or down; left or right!

```
O R F L O W E R S A E C
T C A N D Y Q U E A S A
F D I K T A U A P W T S
C P R I N C E S S O O T
N R Y N S A E A E B A L
K I S G A N N B W N V E
L N A F M N R O C I N U
O C I G A M O S I A O R
Z E A E R O S T A R S I
```

UNICORN   CANDY   KING
RAINBOW   MAGIC   QUEEN
FAIRY   FLOWERS   PRINCESS
CASTLE   STARS   PRINCE

A-maze-ing!

Help this unicorn find her way through the cupcake to the cherry on top!

Find the Unicorn and Uni-Kitty Names

To figure out each name, find the letter that corresponds to each number/letter clue.

	1	2	3	4	5	6
A	Q	Y	J	C	B	T
B	R	D	S	X	F	K
C	P	C	K	G	L	N
D	H	M	L	A	E	U
E	D	A	R	W	O	M
F	N	Z	Y	H	I	V

B3	C1	D4	E3	B6	A2

B3	D1	D4	E2	F2	A4

	1	2	3	4	5	6
A	Y	Q	Z	Y	H	N
B	I	D	P	T	F	P
C	H	P	E	S	G	V
D	E	M	K	A	U	B
E	X	C	P	L	C	G
F	J	H	R	W	L	M

Color the Underwater Scene

Spot the Differences!

There are ten differences between these two rainbow gardens. Can you spot them?

Complete this illustration and then add color.

Flower Garden Word Search

Find all the flowers in the fairy garden.
Look up or down; left or right!

```
        D N A E
      F I O D C L L E
    B A A I N N I Z S A
    A S T E R B A D N M S P
    R Y S I A D K O Y R D E
    O A I S F V B F X T N O
    S A R E W O L F N U S N
    E D I H C R O A I L H Y
    U B E D R G D K I G
    L I L Y S N A P     I
        A R T U
```

TULIP   PANSY   IRIS
DAISY   PEONY   ZINNIA
DAFFODIL   LILY   ORCHID
ROSE   SUNFLOWER   ASTER

Color by Number

Color the garden picture using the color key below!

 1 2 3 4 5 6 7 8

Answer Key

Page 3

Page 5

Page 6

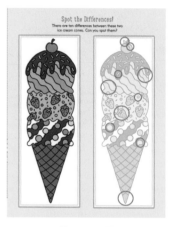

Page 7

Page 9

Page 12

Page 13

Page 14

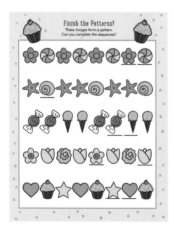

Page 15

Page 16

Page 17

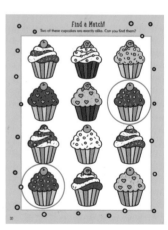

Page 20

Page 21

Page 22

Page 23

Page 26

Page 28

Page 30

Page 31

Page 32

Page 33

Page 34

Page 36

Page 37

Page 38

Page 39

Page 41

Page 47

Page 49

Page 51

Page 54

Page 55

Page 56

Page 58

Page 60

Page 61

We hope you enjoyed this activity book!
Check out other fun books at www.peterpauper.com